ORIGHMI

— CREATIONS —

h

hinkler

hinkler

Published by Hinkler Books Pty Ltd
45–55 Fairchild Street
Heatherton Victoria 3202 Australia
www.hinkler.com.au

Design, layout, cover & photography © Hinkler Books Pty Ltd 2008, 2014, 2016
Text, models & folding techniques © Matthew Gardiner and contributing artists 2008
Paper designs © Shutterstock.com

Author: Matthew Gardiner
Cover design: Sam Grimmer
Cover photography: Ned Meldrum

ISBN: 978 1 4889 3043 0

Printed and bound in China

CONTENTS

ABOUT ORIGAMI

What is origami?

Origami is a curious sounding word because it is not English, but Japanese in origin. Ori, from the root verb oru, means 'to fold' and kami is one of the many terms for paper. In the purest renditions, origami creates an intended shape from a single sheet of paper with no cutting, gluing, taping or any other fastening device allowed. To create less rigid versions one may make small cuts as in kirigami (cut paper) or long slits as in senbazuru – where a single sheet is effectively divided into a number of smaller, still connected squares.

The origin of origami

No-one really knows when origami was invented. We do know that paper had to be invented first, so we can safely say that it is less than 2000 years old, but an exact date, even to the nearest century, cannot be authentically established. Despite its Japanese name, some claim that it is Chinese in origin; this cannot be entirely discounted since many art forms now claimed by others can be traced back to mainland China.

One reason for origami's hazy history is that for many centuries there was almost no documentation on how to do it. The oldest book known to contain origami-like instructions, the Kanamodo, is from the 17th century, yet older woodblock prints show paper folding. The oldest origami book written for leisure is the *Hiden Senbazuru Orikata* from 1797. The title roughly translated means 'the secret technique of folding one thousand cranes'. There are around one hundred designs known as 'traditional origami', which were passed from hand to hand in Japanese culture: typically a mother showing a child, or children sharing among themselves. In fact, until the middle of the 20th century, origami was thought of as something that women did as decorations for weddings, funerals and other ceremonial occasions, or something that young children did as a recreational pursuit.

After the Second World War people from around the world started to visit Japan in greater numbers, and Japanese citizens increased their travel to other countries. Unwittingly, this innocent pastime started to spread around the world, especially with exchange students – those young ambassadors of Japanese culture. The intrepid exchange students could communicate through origami. A finished model could be given as a gift, cementing a friendship through paper folding.

How to Fold

BY: Matthew Gardiner

The key to high quality origami is the quality of each fold. There are many kinds of folds, but the principles described below can be applied to most folds. Origami paper has a coloured side and a white side. When diagrams refer to the coloured side, it is to indicate which colour will be the dominant colour in the final model.

1

Gently lift the bottom corner to the top corner. Don't crease yet, just hold the paper in position.

2

Line up the corners exactly. The image above is not aligned correctly.

3

The corners are exactly aligned; there is no visible difference.

4

Hold the corner with one hand, and slide the forefinger of the other hand down to the bottom.

5

Crease from the centre to the edge. Check that the crease goes exactly through the corner.

6

Crease from the centre to the edge on the other side to complete the fold.

In these two introductory folds, the edges and corners are the references. Use existing creases, corners, edges, intersections of creases, and points to make sure your fold is accurate.

1

Lift the bottom edge to the top edge.

2

Align the corners and then align the edges on one side.

3

Align the opposite corner and edges so that both sides are perfectly aligned.

4

Hold one corner and crease from the centre to the edge.

5
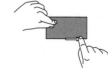

Crease from the centre to the other edge so all corners and edges are aligned.

SYMBOLS

BY: MATTHEW GARDINER

LINES

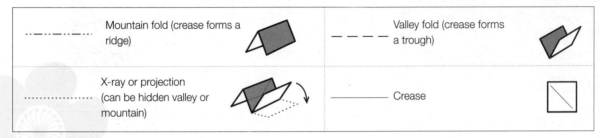

—·—·—·—	Mountain fold (crease forms a ridge)	— — — —	Valley fold (crease forms a trough)
·············	X-ray or projection (can be hidden valley or mountain)	————	Crease

ARROWS

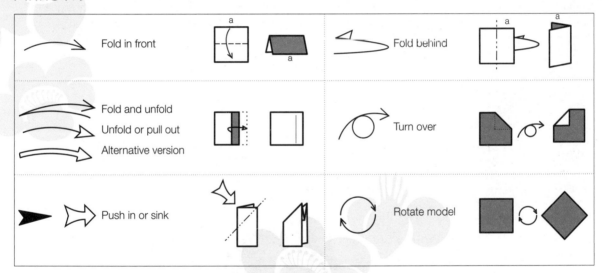

	Fold in front		Fold behind
	Fold and unfold / Unfold or pull out / Alternative version		Turn over
	Push in or sink		Rotate model

EXTRAS

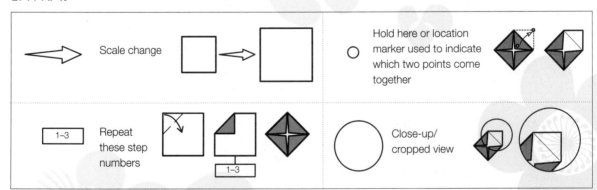

	Scale change	○	Hold here or location marker used to indicate which two points come together
1–3	Repeat these step numbers		Close-up/cropped view

6

TYPES OF FOLDS

BY: MATTHEW GARDINER

BOOK FOLD

Valley fold one edge to another, like closing a book.

CUPBOARD FOLD

Fold both edges to the middle crease, like closing two cupboard doors.

BLINTZ FOLD

Fold all corners to the middle. This was named after a style of pastry called a blintz.

INSIDE REVERSE FOLD

The spine of the existing fold is reversed and pushed inside.

OUTSIDE REVERSE FOLD

The spine of the existing fold is reversed and wrapped outside.

PETAL FOLD   The petal fold is found in the crane and lily base.

1	2	3	4	5
Fold top layer to the centre crease.	Fold and unfold the top triangle down. Unfold flaps.	Lift the top layer upwards.	Step 3 in progress, the model is 3D. Fold the top layer inwards on existing creases.	Completed petal fold.

SQUASH FOLD   A squash fold is the symmetrical flattening of a point. The flattening movement is known as squashing the point.

1	2	3	4
Pre-crease on the line for the squash fold.	Open up the paper by inserting your finger. Fold the paper across.	As you put the paper in place, gently squash the point into a symmetrical shape.	Completed squash fold.

PAPER CRANE

MODEL: TRADITIONAL, JAPAN
DIAGRAM: MATTHEW GARDINER

The traditional Japanese paper crane or *orizuru* is famous throughout the world. It is a symbol of origami and a symbol of peace. An ancient Japanese legend says that whoever folds 1000 cranes will be granted a wish.

Today, in Hiroshima, stands the peace memorial of Sadako Sasaki built by her classmates in her memory to inspire peace around the world. Sadako was a victim of 'atomic bomb disease' and she folded cranes until she died. She never gave up on her wish to be well.

1

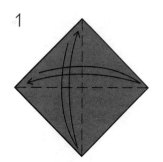

Start coloured side up.
Fold and unfold diagonals.
Turn over.

2

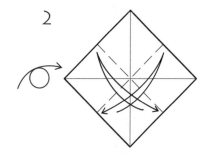

Book fold and unfold.

3

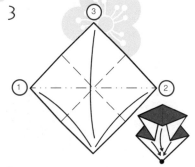

Bring three corners down to meet bottom corner. Start with corners 1 and 2 together followed by corner 3.

4

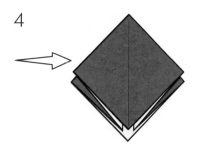

Completed preliminary base.

5

Fold top layer to the centre crease.

6

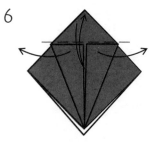

Fold and unfold the top triangle down. Unfold flaps.

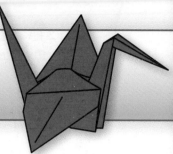

7

Lift the top layer upwards.

8

Step 7 in progress, the model is 3D. Fold the top layer inwards on existing creases.

9

Step 7 completed, the model will be flat. Turn over.

10

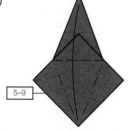

5–9

Repeat steps 5–9 on this side.

11

Narrow the bottom points on the top layer only. Repeat behind.

12

Reverse fold the bottom point upwards.

13

Your model should look like this. Repeat on the other side.

14

Completed body. The next steps focus on the head.

15

Reverse fold the point to create the head.

9

THE PAPER CRANE

MODEL: TRADITIONAL, JAPAN
DIAGRAM: MATTHEW GARDINER

16

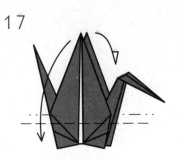

Head completed.

17

Fold wings down.

18

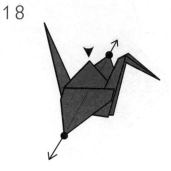

Pull the wings gently to shape the body.

19

Completed paper crane – repeat 1000 times for a wish.

WATER LILY

MODEL: TRADITIONAL, JAPAN
DIAGRAM: MATTHEW GARDINER

The water lily is a beautiful form, invoking the charm of the lily floating on the water.

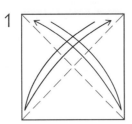

1

Fold and unfold diagonals.

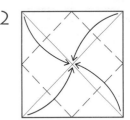

2

Fold corners to the centre.

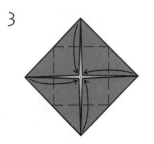

3

Fold corners to the centre again.

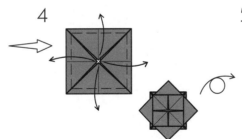

4

Fold indicated corners outwards leaving a small gap at the edges. Turn over.

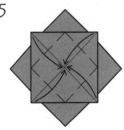

5

While folding the indicated corners to the centre, the model will change into 3D.

6

Completed step 5. Turn over.

7

Fold indicated corners outside leaving a little gap at the edges. Turn over.

8

Completed water lily.

BUTTERFLY

MODEL: TRADITIONAL, JAPAN
DIAGRAM: MATTHEW GARDINER

Butterflies capture the imagination of children and adults alike. Their delicate shape is perfect for hanging decorations. Try using a patterned sheet of origami paper.

1

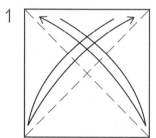

Fold and unfold diagonals.

2

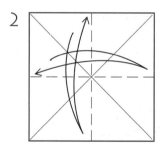

Book fold and fold.

3

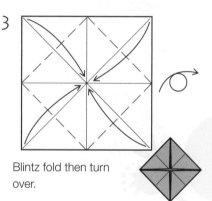

Blintz fold then turn over.

4

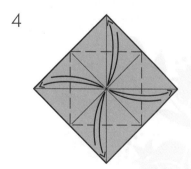

Blintz fold then turn over.

5

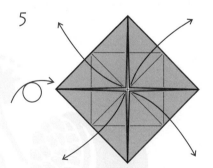

Completely unfold out to a flat sheet.

6

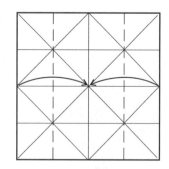

Fold sides to the middle.

7

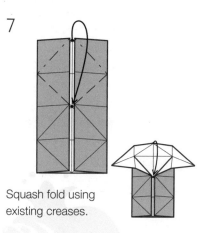

Squash fold using existing creases.

8

9

Repeat step 7 on the bottom.

Mountain fold in half.

10

11

12

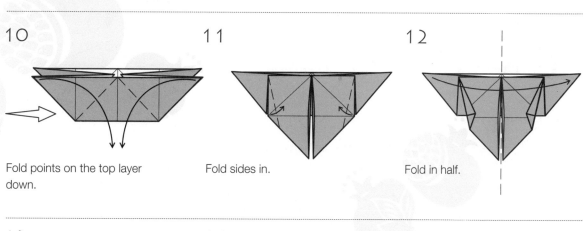

Fold points on the top layer down.

Fold sides in.

Fold in half.

13

14

15

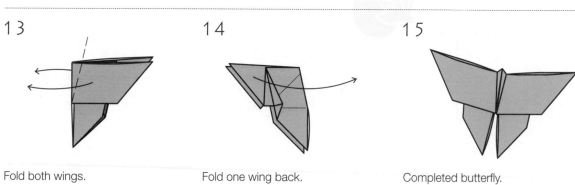

Fold both wings.

Fold one wing back.

Completed butterfly.

FISH

MODEL: TRADITIONAL, JAPAN
DIAGRAM: MATTHEW GARDINER

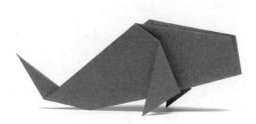

Fish are adored by the Japanese, both as a food and as a symbol of health, vitality and energy. A Japanese annual festival for boys uses the highly spirited carp (koi) as a symbol for energy and power. Look above the rooftops in late April to early May in Japan and you will see paper and cloth fish flying high. One fish per boy in the household is flown. Use a bright colour for this origami fish.

1
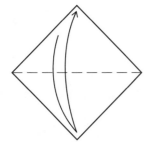

Start with white side up. Fold and unfold diagonal.

2
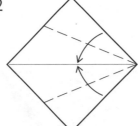

Fold both sides to the middle.

3
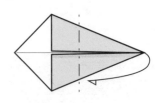

Mountain fold in half behind.

4
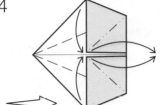

Squash fold both sides.

5

Mountain fold the back layer behind.

6
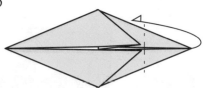

This is known as the fish base. Mountain fold the point.

7

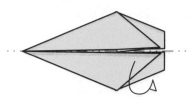

Mountain fold in half behind.

8

Fold the fins down on both sides.

9

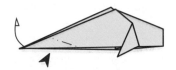

Inside reverse fold the tail.

10

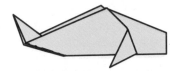

Completed fish.

FOX

MODEL: TRADITIONAL, JAPAN
DIAGRAM: MATTHEW GARDINER

The fox is a cunning creature. In Japanese mythology, foxes possess magical abilities and wisdom, and some have the ability to change into human form. This fox is a fun little hand puppet that gives the wearer special fox abilities. Use this puppet with care, and respect the animals of the world.

The Japanese say that a sunshower (rain falling from a clear sky) is the sign of a fox wedding.

1

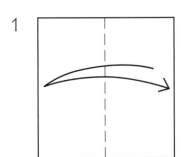

Book fold and unfold.

2

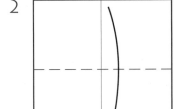

Book fold.

3

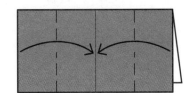

Cupboard fold.

4

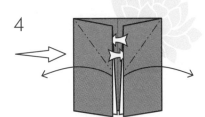

Open up the pocket and squash fold.

5

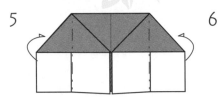

Mountain fold sides.

6

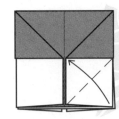

Fold up corner of top layer.

7

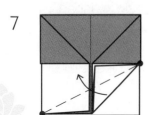

Fold up.

8

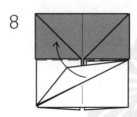

Fold up again.
Turn over.

9

Fold up corner.

10

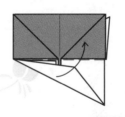

Fold up.

11

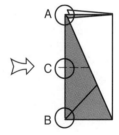

Fold up again.

12

90°

A
C
B

Push point C further in so
point A and B touch.

13

Completed fox.

14

Insert your hand in the back
and use as a puppet.

TATO

MODEL: TRADITIONAL, JAPAN
DIAGRAM: MATTHEW GARDINER

The tato is a form of paper purse or puzzle in Japan. Tatogami is a folded paper that is used to store expensive kimonos, however this tato design is for smaller objects. Origami masters Shuzo Fujimoto and Michio Uchiyama are renowned for their innovation in expanding tato designs. The primary method involves dividing the square radially, in this case into eight segments, that fold inward over each other.

Tato can be folded from fabric, or two laminated sheets of paper for maximum durability and effect.

1

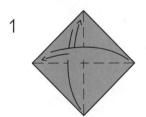

Start coloured side up.
Fold and unfold diagonals.
Turn over.

2

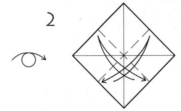

Book fold and unfold.

3

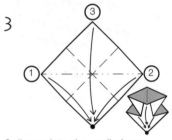

Collapse into the preliminary base.

4

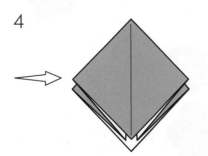

The preliminary base.

5

Fold edges of top layer to the centre.

6

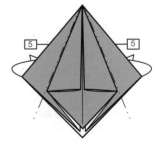

Repeat step 5 on the other side.

7

Unfold to a flat sheet.

8

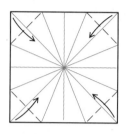

Fold corners in at the intersection of existing creases. This makes a perfect octagon.

9

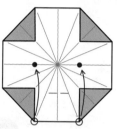

Fold the edge to the middle. Be careful to only crease as shown.

10

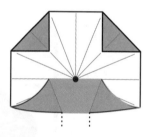

Step 9 in process. Only crease between the dotted lines.

11

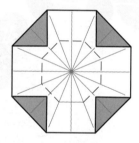

Repeat step 9 all around the octagon.

12

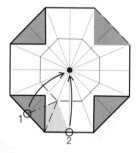

Fold point 1 to the middle. Then fold point 2. This will create a point with the greyed-out paper. Fold this point to the left. Look ahead to step 13 to see the result.

13

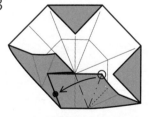

Fold the point marked by the circle to the point marked by the dot.

14

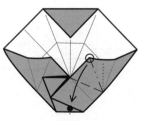

Repeat step 13 on the remaining points. The last point needs to be tucked under the first point.

15

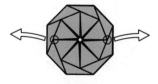

The finished tato. To open the purse gently pull on two opposite points.

WALKING CRAB

MODEL: SHOKO AOYAGI
DIAGRAM: SHOKO AOYAGI

The walking crab is a fun design that walks sideways when you tap it. Shoko Aoyagi is well known for her fun origami style – she likes to use stick-on eyes to add character to her origami creations. You cut out circles of white and black paper and glue them together, or use pre-cut circles that are available at office-supply stores.

The walking crab is a contemporary Japanese design.

1

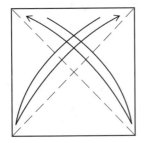

Fold and unfold diagonals. Turn over.

2

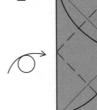

Blintz fold.

3

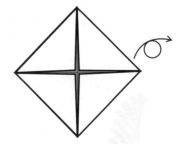

Completed step 2. Turn over.

4

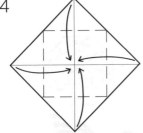

Blintz fold again.

5

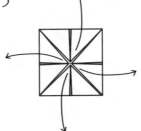

Completely unfold the paper.

6

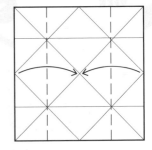

Cupboard fold.

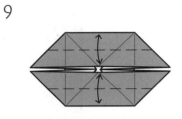

7

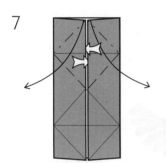

Bring both corners forwards and squash fold.

8

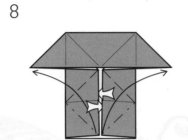

Repeat step 7 on other end.

9

Fold and unfold top and bottom edge to the centre.

10

Open up pockets.

11

This shows the pockets open. Lift up inside corners, and fold the edges outwards.

12

Fold edge to corner.

13

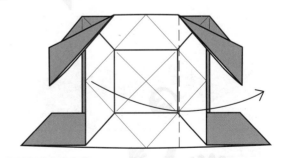

Fold over.

14

Fold over.

15

Fold in half through all layers.

16

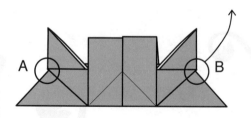

Hold point A with one hand. Pull point B upwards.

17

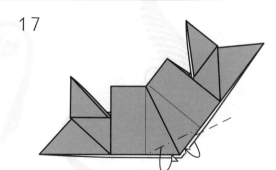

Fold inside the base of the front flap as shown. Repeat on the other side.

18

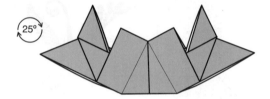

Completed walking crab.

19

When you tap point C, the crab will walk sideways. Attach round stickers for eyes and draw eyeballs.

SWAN

MODEL: TRADITIONAL, JAPAN
DIAGRAM: MATTHEW GARDINER

This simple origami swan expresses the form of this elegant bird swimming on the water of a lake.

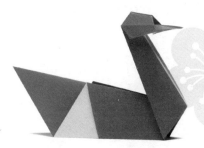

1

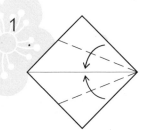

Pre-crease diagonal. Fold sides to the middle.

2

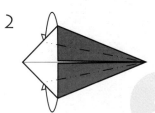

Mountain fold both sides to the middle.

3

Fold in half.

4

Outside reverse fold the neck.

5

Outside reverse fold the head.

6

Pull out hidden paper on both sides of the head.

7

Pleat, then double reverse fold the head to form the beak.

8

Completed swan.

IRIS

MODEL: TRADITIONAL, JAPAN
DIAGRAM: MATTHEW GARDINER

The iris takes its name from the Greek word for rainbow. Its name reflects the wide range of colours of the iris. This model looks best when folded from a blended or two-toned paper.

The iris is a popular symbol, appearing on the flag of Brussels, and in the fleur-de-lis, the symbol of Florence, Italy.

1

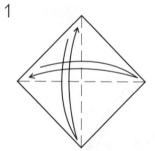

Fold and unfold diagonals. Turn over.

2

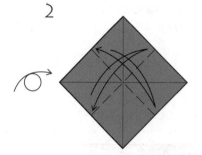

Book fold and unfold.

3

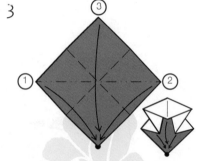

Bring three corners down to meet bottom corner. Start with corners 1 and 2 together followed by corner 3.

4

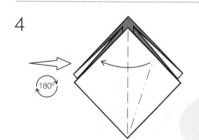

Pre-crease then squash fold.

5

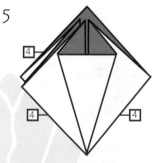

Repeat step 4 on the other three sides.

6

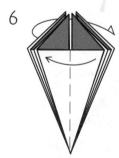

Turn top and back layer over.

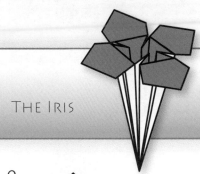

7

Fold top layer edges to meet the middle.

8

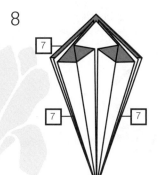

Repeat step 7 to both sides and behind.

9

Fold front petal down.

10

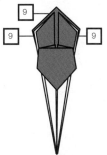

Repeat step 9 on all three sides, making the model 3D. Start with both side petals followed by the back petal.

11

Completed iris.

25

LILY

Follow the instructions for the iris on the previous page up to step 7, but start with the coloured side up.

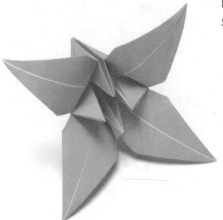

1

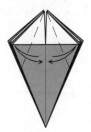

Start from step 7 of the iris. Fold the top layer only to the centre crease.

2

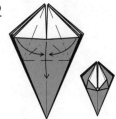

Petal fold; pull down the top layer, and fold the sides to the middle. Lastly, make the mountain folds.

3

Completed petal fold. Fold the triangle flap upwards.

4

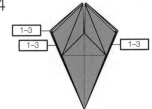

Repeat steps 1–3 on the three remaining sides.

5

Fold one layer in front and behind.

6

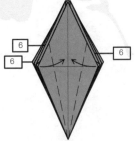

Fold edges to the middle, thinning the lily. Repeat on the other three sides.

7

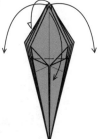

Make a soft, curved valley fold on all four sides to open out the lily.

8

Completed lily.

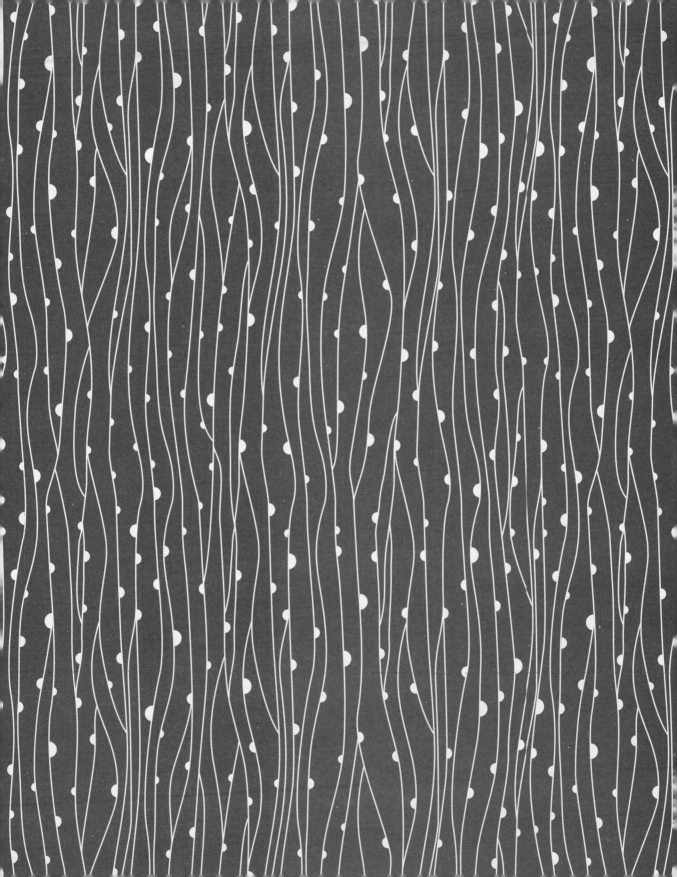

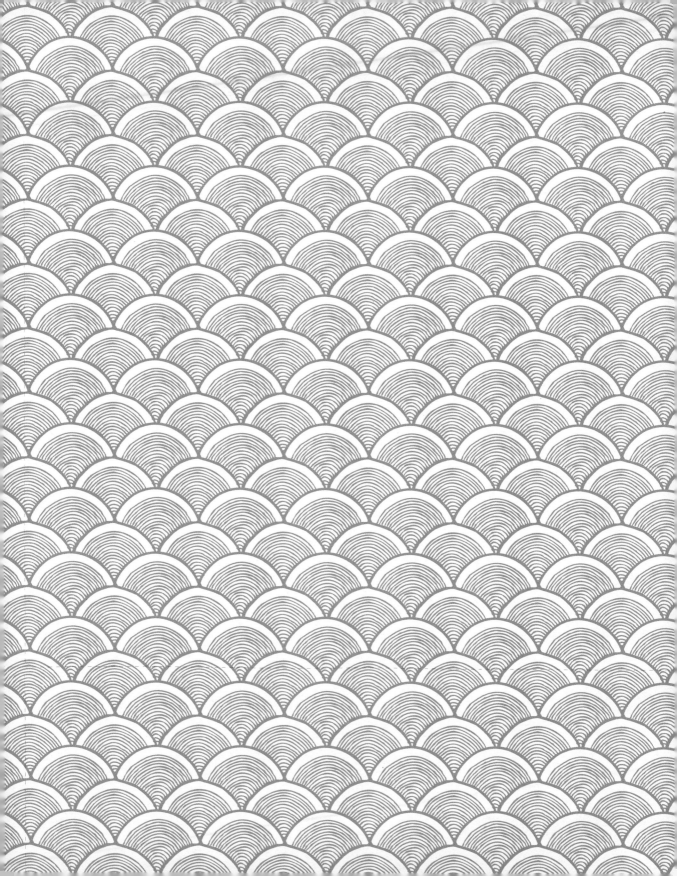

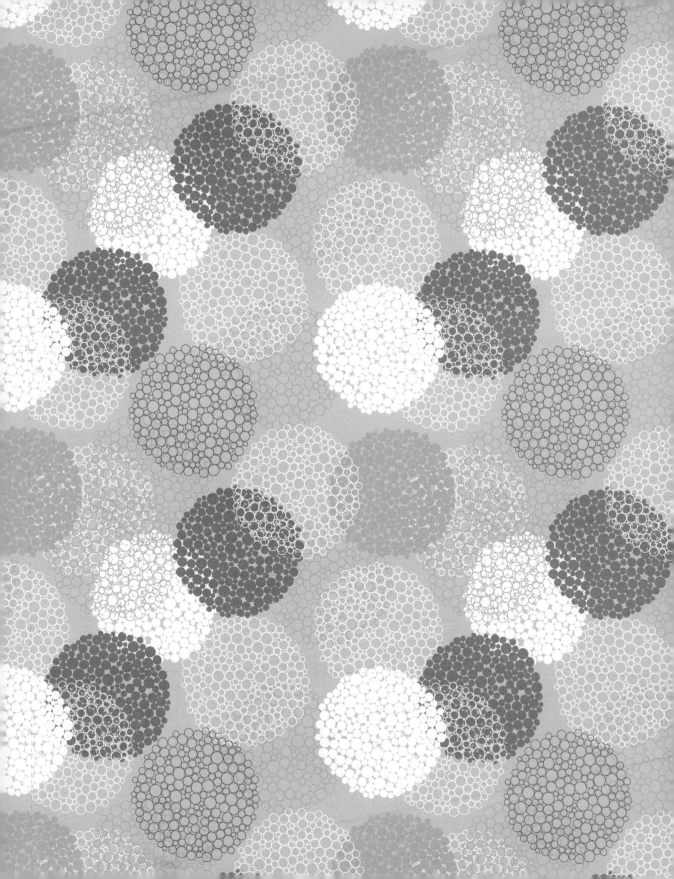

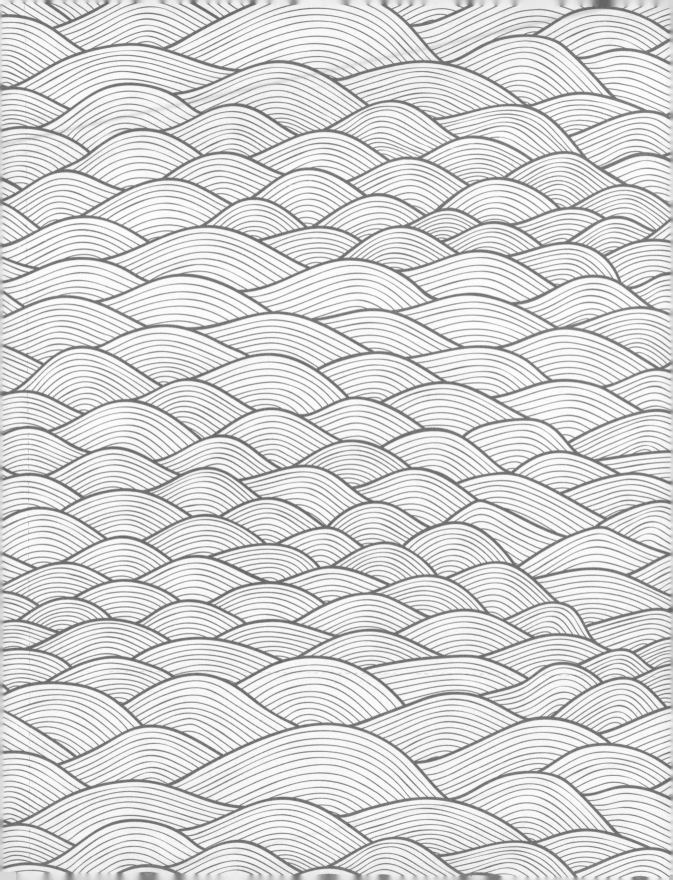

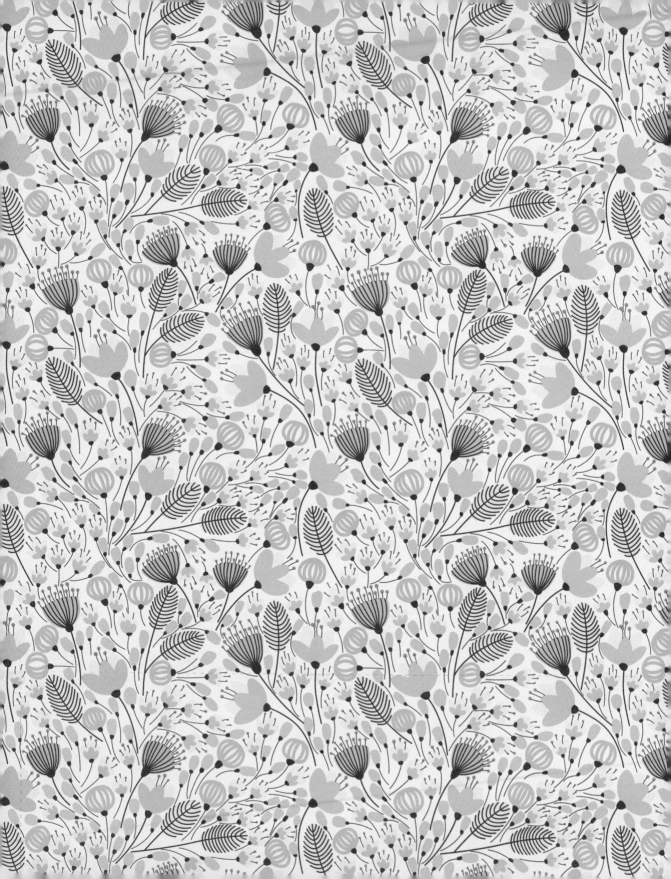

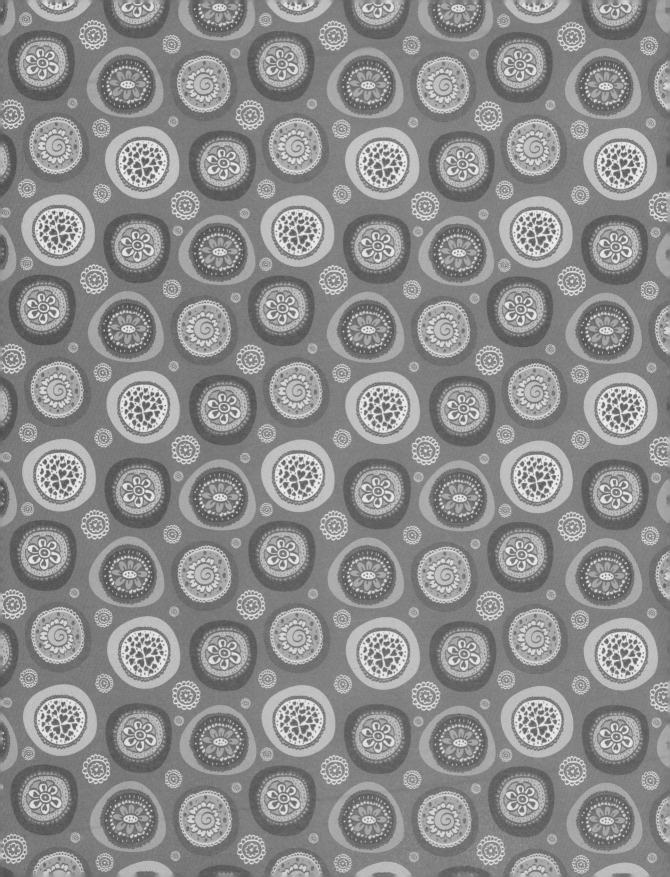

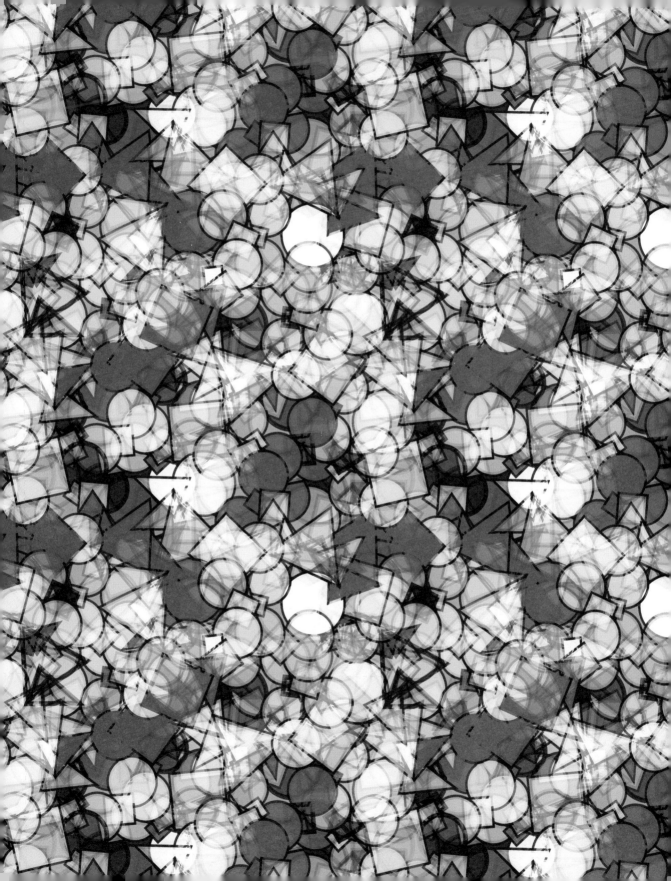